Quotable

Wooden

Quotable
Wooden

WORDS OF WISDOM, PREPARATION, AND SUCCESS BY AND ABOUT JOHN WOODEN, COLLEGE BASKETBALL'S GREATEST COACH

John Reger

TowleHouse Publishing
Nashville, Tennessee

TowleHouse books are distributed by National Book Network (NBN),
4720 Boston Way, Lanham, Maryland 20706.

Library of Congress Cataloging-in-Publication data is available.
ISBN: 1-931249-09-1

Cover design by Gore Studio, Inc.
Page design by Mike Towle

Printed in the United States of America
1 2 3 4 5 6 — 06 05 04 03 02

CONTENTS

ACKNOWLEDGMENTS

T he staff at UCLA's Sports Information Department was extremely helpful, especially Marc Dellins, Bill Bennett, and Steve Rourke. They are the easiest, most professional people one could ask for in researching a project like this. My deepest gratitude is extended to them.

Thanks also to Elliot Bloom at Purdue University's Athletic Public Relations Office for assisting in a last-minute request.

I would not have done this book if it weren't for Michael Arkush, who had the faith in me to make the key introduction.

Lastly, my wife, Marianne, who puts up with the late nights alone and the weekends apart so I can chase dreams. In my quest to light the world on fire with my talent, she makes sure that I don't burn my fingers.

PREFACE

Though my name is given author's credit on this book, these will be the only words I write. What follows in this book are words spoken at one time or another by John Robert Wooden or about him by family, players, coaches, and friends.

My task was to select the best ones, and while Wooden himself said perfection is impossible, its pursuit should never be stopped. When I covered UCLA athletics, Wooden had been retired for more than twenty years. The signs of his impact were evident and one could not walk into Pauley Pavilion and not notice the ten NCAA Championship banners hanging from the rafters.

What is more difficult to find is the mark left by Wooden off the basketball court. His success in that arena is far more admirable, though much less chronicled.

While sociologists and other experts debate why our children are so ill equipped to live in the world—and who bears the responsibility for that failure—I present Joshua Wooden as evidence for a longstanding theory. John Wooden's father was a modest man rich in principles and guidance that he passed on to his four boys. Many of John Wooden's tenets for his Pyramid of Success and other teachings were laid on the foundation built by his father.

Like his father, Wooden puts family first, followed by his faith and then his friends. The two people he admires most are Abraham Lincoln and Mother Teresa. One of his favorite sayings came from Mother Teresa: "A life not lived for others is not a life."

Wooden mirrors that maxim, and his teachings have affected everyone who has come in contact with him. Directly or indirectly, he has taught hundreds how to be better people, and he took no credit for doing so. My hope is that this book gives him some recognition for the lives he has touched, including mine. This world would be a better place if there were more human beings like John Wooden.

THE INDIANA
YEARS

"I coached scared then, as most new coaches do when they're starting."

—JOHN WOODEN

My first basketball was one
my mother made. She
took an old sock, made it
as round as possible, and
covered it with rags.[1]

~

I practiced so much at the hoop I put up at home when I was a kid that after a while I could literally shoot free throws in the dark and make them.[2]

〜

JOHNNY, WE COULD HAVE WON WITH YOU IN THERE, BUT WINNING JUST ISN'T THAT IMPORTANT.
> —*Earl Warriner, Wooden's coach at Centerton Grade School, who benched Wooden despite his being the team's star player*

〜

On a farm you are brought up with a work ethic that a lot of people don't get. I think that helped me. I learned a lot of lessons.

〜

They called me "the Indiana Rubber Man" in high
school because every time I went down on the court I
bounced right back up.

⌒

WHEN THEY REVISE THE NEW TESTAMENT, THERE'LL BE A
CHAPTER IN THERE ABOUT JOHN R. WOODEN.
                    —*Floyd Burns, friend and teammate from Martinsville High*

⌒

The greatest shot I ever saw.
                    —*talking about an opponent's underhanded scoop*
                    shot that defeated Wooden's Martinsville High, 13-12, in
                    the 1928 Indiana State School Championships in his senior year

⌒

"The Indiana Rubber Man" during his playing days at Purdue. (Photo courtesy of ASUCLA Photography)

When the buzzer signaled the end of that game, one
that is still talked about by old-time Indiana basketball fans, most of my teammates broke down and
cried. I did not. I believed I had done the best I
could. I had prepared and played hard and knew it.
                              —*after a 13-12 loss to Muncie Central in
                              the 1928 Indiana State School Championship*

JOHNNY WOODEN, ALL-TIME ALL-AMERICAN, A PLAYER OF
RENOWN AND FAME, STREAKING UP AND DOWN THE HARD-
WOOD, LIKE A BOLT OF BURNING FLAME.
                              —*Stanley Jacobs, basketball manager at South Bend
                              Central High, writing about Wooden's playing days*

With all my belongings in one suitcase and a dollar or
two in my pocket, some friends drove me to West
Lafayette, where I hoped to be good enough to play
basketball and smart enough to get my degree.[3]

He was my role model. He knew the entire game
and taught it with consummate skill. I always thought
he was years ahead of his time and that I was very
fortunate to have played for him.

—*on his Purdue coach, Ward "Piggie" Lambert*

I PLAYED FOR HIM FOR FOUR YEARS, AND I DON'T REMEM-
BER HIM EVER BRAGGING ABOUT HIS OWN PLAYING DAYS.

—*Mike Lynn, a former player*

I ATTRIBUTE JOHN'S SUCCESS TO THE FACT THAT HE WAS
ALWAYS MOTIVATED.[4]

—*Maurice Wooden, Wooden's brother*

I coached scared then, as most new coaches do when
they're starting.

—*on his first coaching job*

BASICALLY HE WAS TOUGH.[5]

—Lenny Rzeszewski, who played for Wooden at
South Bend Central and Indiana State University

⌢

ELKHART SCHOOL OFFICIALS ANNOUNCED TODAY THAT
JOHN WOODEN, ENGLISH TEACHER AND COACH OF SOUTH
BEND CENTRAL HIGH SCHOOL, WOULD BE THE PRINCIPAL
SPEAKER AT THEIR RECOGNITION DINNER, ALTHOUGH THEY
HAD HOPED TO GET A PROMINENT PERSON.

—announcement in 1946 Elkhart Truth *newspaper*

⌢

During those early days, baseball was really my
favorite. All of the boys loved it so Dad leveled off one
end of a field and made a baseball diamond for us.[6]

⌢

Wooden played pro basketball on weekends and received fifty dollars a game, more than any other player in the country during the 1930s:

I never did it for the money. I don't think any of us did. We did it purely because we loved the game. To me, that's what playing professional basketball meant. Those were good times . . . great times.[7]

To this day, I have never seen a team play better team basketball. They had great athletes, but they weren't as impressive as their team play. The way they handled and passed the ball was just amazing to me then, and I believe it would be today.[8]

—*describing the New York Renaissance, the first all-black professional basketball team. Wooden played against the Rens when he was a member of the barnstorming Indianapolis Kautskys during the thirties.*

2

THE EARLY WESTWOOD DAYS

"I have never played on or coached a losing team and I don't intend to start now."

—JOHN WOODEN

My first impression of UCLA, on my visit, had not been good. I was appalled at the facilities. That was probably the reason I preferred Minnesota. They had a huge fieldhouse while UCLA had a tiny gym that later became known as the B.O. Barn when we began to fill it to the ceiling.[1]

WOODEN WILL MAKE AN EXCELLENT ADDITION TO THE UCLA COACHING STAFF. HE'S A REAL GENTLEMAN AND COACH.
—*Wilbur Johns, then the UCLA athletic director, on Wooden's 1948 hiring*

I have never played on or coached a losing team and I don't intend to start now.
—*on the opening day of his first season at UCLA*

I can't say one way or the other whether I'm pleased or displeased with what I found when I walked on the UCLA basketball court. I'll tell you one thing, though. No team is going to outrun or outhustle the Bruins this season.

～

When I went up on the floor for the first time in the spring of 1948 and put them through that first practice, I was very disappointed. I felt that my Indiana State team could have named the score against them. I was shattered. Had I known how to abort the agreement in an honorable manner, I would have done so and gone to Minnesota, or, if that was impossible, stayed on at Indiana State.[2]

～

TAKING OVER ONLY AN AVERAGE GROUP OF BOYS, JOVIAL
JOHN PROCEEDED TO BAMBOOZLE THE WORLD OF SPORTS BY
PRODUCING THE SCRAPPIEST AGGREGATION OF LANKY LEMS
EVER TO SET FOOT ON A BRUIN HARDBOARD PATCH. TO
COACH WOODEN, A TOPFLIGHT LEADER IN THE KNOW-HOW
DEPARTMENT AND A STERLING PERSONALITY IF EVER THERE
WAS ONE, UCLA HAS ALREADY DOFFED ITS HAT. HAIL THE
CONQUERING HERO, AND WATCH FOR THINGS TO COME!
—UCLA *Yearbook*, 1949

In my early years as coach, I ran a pretty taut ship.
Every detail was spelled out from the cut of the
player's hair to the style of dress for games.[3]

I wanted a better place to play, but it didn't displease
me that the other teams dreaded to come in there.
—*on the tiny campus gym known as the B.O. Barn.*

I was not at ease in Southern California. Frankly, I came from the farm and Los Angeles was frightening to me.

I was not totally enthralled with UCLA,

Despite the fact that the first two years had been fairly successful, I was not totally enthralled with UCLA, and it was about this time that various representatives from Purdue were talking to me about going back to West Lafayette. They made a tremendous offer—a lot better financially than the six thousand dollars I got to come to UCLA.[4]

I don't like recruiting. I don't like the idea of trying to sell someone on something. I'd never be a salesman.

Wooden had the regal look of a champion long before UCLA's basketball dynasty was practically a given. (Photo courtesy of ASUCLA Photography)

A lot of these players after they did pretty well, they'll say they were recruited tremendously. Not one of them was highly recruited.[5]

—on his 1964 NCAA Championship team

⁓

I never dreamed about winning a national championship; it happened before I even thought it was possible.[6]

⁓

I can honestly say that I received more criticism after we won a championship than I did before we won one. That's why I've always said I wish all my really good friends in coaching would win one national championship and those I don't think highly of, I wish they would win several.

⁓

There is a very fine line between the champion and the runner-up. Six or seven of my teams, in my opinion, had the potential to win the NCAA championship before the 1964 team succeeded.[7]

Now you are the champions and you must act like champions. You meet some people going up. You will meet the same people going down.[8]

—*addressing one of his championship teams*

THE PRACTICES

"We thought he was a lunatic.
We thought he was a walking antique."

—BILL WALTON

I enjoyed planning and conducting practices. That was one of my strengths. I equated coaching with Cervantes, who said, "The journey is better than the inn."

I used to tell my players, "My job is the two hours I have you on the floor for practice every day. Your job is what you do between those practices, because you can tear down faster than we can build up by lack of moderation."

We didn't have any drills where you just stand and shoot. Players were constantly moving. Every fundamental drill was a conditioning drill.

If the players weren't focusing in practice, I'd say, "That's it. Out. Come back tomorrow and be ready to go." Almost always they'd say, "Give us another chance." And almost always, practice would go fine after that.[1]

It is impossible to attain proper physical condition without being sound both mentally and morally.

If I am through learning, I am through.

It's what you learn after you know it all that counts.

The only place that success is before work is in the dictionary.

~

Failure to prepare is preparing to fail.

~

If you don't have time to do it right, when will you have time to do it over?

~

Learn as if you were going to live forever, and live as if you were going to die tomorrow.

~

WE THOUGHT HE WAS A LUNATIC. WE THOUGHT
HE WAS A WALKING ANTIQUE. WE THOUGHT,
"WHAT'S ALL THIS STUFF YOU'RE TALKING
ABOUT?" BE QUICK, BUT DON'T HURRY. FAILING TO
PREPARE IS PREPARING TO FAIL. DON'T EVER BEAT
YOURSELF; IT'S THE WORST KIND OF DEFEAT
YOU'LL SUFFER. ALL THOSE THINGS HE WOULD
TELL US ALL THE TIME. WE DIDN'T REALIZE HE WAS
RIGHT ON THE MARK UNTIL WE STARTED TO LOSE.[2]

—*Bill Walton*

I used the bench to teach. When future two-time
All-American Walt Hazzard first came to us at
UCLA, he had a tendency to get a little fancy. He
didn't continue being fancy because he liked to play.[3]

I felt that running a practice session was almost like
teaching an English class in that I wanted to have a
lesson plan. I knew the detailed plan was necessary in
teaching English, but it took a while before I understood the same thing was necessary in sports.[4]

People usually know what they should do to get
what they want. They just won't do it. They
won't pay the price.[5]

Don't measure yourself by what you have accomplished but by what you should have accomplished with your ability.

⌒

Like most coaches, my program revolved around fundamentals, conditioning, and teamwork. But I differed radically in several respects. I never worried about how our opponents would play us, and I never talked about winning.

⌒

I felt if we prepared fully we would do just fine. If we won, great; frosting on the cake. But at no time did I consider winning to be the cake.[6]

⌒

I seldom punished players at practice or in front of others. Some coaches believe in giving laps or sprints for errors. I don't think that works. I'm not sure how the body chemistry functions precisely, but I doubt that it responds properly to punishment of that type.[7]

———

At the first squad meeting each season, held two weeks before our first actual practice, I personally demonstrated how I wanted players to put on their socks each and every time. I would watch as the player smoothed the sock under and along the back of the heel. I wanted it done conscientiously, not quickly or casually. I wanted absolutely no folds, wrinkles, or creases of any kind on the sock. I would demonstrate for the players and then have the players demonstrate for me. This may seem like a nuisance, trivial, but I had a very practical reason for being meticulous about this. Wrinkles, folds, and creases can cause blisters. Blisters interfere with performance during practice and games.[8]

———

4

THE GAMES

"The Bruins are like an IBM machine."

—GEORGE RAVELING

THE BRUINS ARE LIKE AN IBM MACHINE. ALL JOHN WOODEN
HAS TO DO IS PUNCH IN *WIN*.

—*George Raveling, basketball coach*

⌒

I probably scouted opponents less than any coach in
the country, less than most high school coaches. I
don't need to know that this forward likes to drive
the outside. You're not supposed to give the outside
to any forward whenever he tries it. Sound offensive
and defensive principles apply to any style of play.

⌒

Rather than having my teams prepare to play a certain team each week, I prepared to play anybody. I
didn't want my players worrying about the other fel-
lows. I wanted them executing the sound offensive
and defensive principles we taught in practice.

⌒

I try to operate on the same
theory at all times, whether I
win or not. I never put pressure
on a player to win. I tell all my
players that if they keep their
heads up and can be satisfied
with themselves, more often
than not they will outscore
the opponent.

"Sid, what's wrong?" Wooden asked.
"I just can't believe we lost," Wicks said.
"Then I suggest not to do it again," Wooden replied.

In the huddle I let them decide what man will shoot. I
know what their decision will be. Only if their decision
disagrees with mine would I over-rule. Almost always
they make the right decision on their own.

I don't want to see it happen, though it's definitely
possible that it will. I would say that as far as next
year is concerned, we will be a better basketball team
after we are beaten, or if we are successful in breaking
the record, we'll be better after it has been broken.
—*after the 1972 season, when UCLA had a forty-five-game
winning streak intact, challenging the University of
San Francisco's NCAA record sixty-game winning streak*

If I have said it once, I have said it a hundred
times, that once we broke the record last year, the
streak became meaningless. I am fairly certain my
players felt this way. I am not mad or glad about
the streak, and my players are acting like they
should—like men.

⌒

Do you want me to say what I really think or what
you want to hear?

—after 71-70 loss at Notre Dame broke the Bruins'
record streak of eighty-eight consecutive victories

⌒

I told them that when you get whipped, you keep
your mouths shut. Let the winners do all the talking.

⌒

Before every game I looked for Nell in the crowd and waved. It was something I had done since my first coaching job. There were some times I had a hard time finding her. It is a nice tradition.

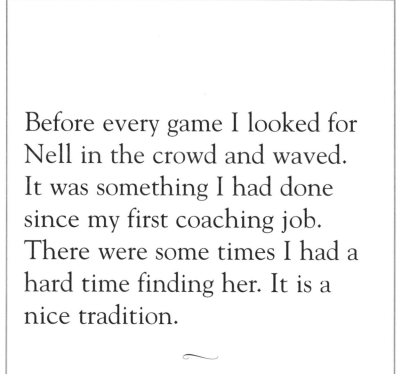

WE'RE REALLY NOT SUPERSTITIOUS. WE JUST DON'T TAKE
ANY CHANCES.

—*Nellie Wooden*

∽

In forty years of coaching, Wooden was called for a technical foul twice:
I never called officials names, and you never heard me
use a word of profanity. I never got personal. I'd say the
worst thing I ever said to an official, and I wouldn't like
somebody to say it to me if I were officiating, was, "Call
them the same on both ends." Or I might say, "Don't be
a homer." To be quite honest with you, although two
were called on me, one really (shouldn't have been)
called on me. The official thought that I said something
that somebody behind me said. But I kept it. I didn't
have any confrontation with him at all in any way.[1]

∽

I would have to say that of all the games I was involved in as a coach, that was the most disappointing loss I've ever had. I don't mean to demean North Carolina State—they were a fine team. But I really felt we were better. We just didn't show it.[2]

—on UCLA's double-overtime, 80-77 loss to North Carolina State in the 1974 Final Four semifinals

WOODEN MADE THESE CHANGES AND IT MADE THEM A MUCH BETTER TEAM THAN WE PLAYED A WEEK AGO. THEY CERTAINLY ADJUSTED VERY WELL TO THE CHANGES IN ONLY ONE WEEK.[3]

—Digger Phelps after a 94-75 loss one week after the same Notre Dame team had stopped UCLA's eighty-eight-game winning streak

5

THE DYNASTY

*"I don't think any of them are
ever as sweet as the first one."*

—JOHN WOODEN

I'm not sure that one school winning so much is good. It creates things like envy, jealousy, and suspicion. This is not good. But that does not mean that I don't want to continue winning. I want to win every game we play. If I didn't, I wouldn't be coaching.

It's better that we're not fawned over. If they made too much of it when we did well, they might make too much of it when we do poorly.[1]

—*talking about the laid-back fans of Southern California*

We're a great college team. If we're the greatest, I don't know because I don't have all the evidence needed to decide. But the pros? Well, you have to realize they have it over us in maturity and depth.

—*after winning the 1968 NCAA Championship*

Every team wants to beat us more today than (before). When a team beats us now, it acts as if it won a national championship.

Wooden's bench demeanor was rarely overly vocal or excessively demonstrative, which would have made him a novelty in today's game. (Photo courtesy of ASUCLA Photography)

No, I don't think we've created a monster by winning so much. Rather than calling what we've achieved a dynasty, I prefer to think of it as a cycle, and I believe all cycles come to an end.[2]

Actually, each team I ever coached had its own particular character. But while I have never said that any one of them was better than another, I guess I'll have to admit to having a special feeling for my first NCAA Championship (1964).[3]

⌒

I don't think any of them are ever as sweet as the first one. It's like a youngster with a first car. No car after that ever means quite as much.

⌒

I don't tell them to beat any opponent by thirty points. But I do tell them during practices and before games that I expect them to do their best.

⌒

I'll have to talk to Bill about the one he missed.

—after Bill Walton made twenty-one of twenty-two
shots from the field en route to forty-four points in the
1973 NCAA Championship, 87-66 victory over Memphis State

It's of small concern to most individuals who wins this tourney anyway.

—after UCLA's ninth championship

The same thing was said about the Yankees in baseball. Whether it's an individual or a team, whenever you reach a plateau of excellence, there are always a lot of people who want to see you knocked down. Then, when that happens, they don't know what they were complaining about. There were those who wanted to see Joe Louis get whipped when he was heavyweight champion all those years. Then, when he did, they were sorry.[4]

I think the significance of UCLA's invincibility was probably heavier in the minds of our opponents than it was in our own minds. And by that time, we believed there was no way we could lose big games, important games, games that would influence conference championships and NCAA Tournaments.[5]

I'm glad we won this year. I finally got a watch for myself. The other five went to my son, my son-in-law, and my three grandsons.

—after winning his sixth NCAA Championship in 1970

As I look back, most everything I have is a result of sport. Oh, I know it's the toy part of the world and I'm not significant in any worldly fashion. But a long time ago I found this niche and it has been right for me. I've enjoyed coaching, teaching, and the relationships . . . I am content. I have peace of mind, and I worry about how much I'm going to miss sport when I get out of it in the near future.[6]

6

THE TEACHER

"Coach taught us self-discipline and was always his own best example."

—KAREEM ABDUL-JABBAR

On the floor I'm not interested in my players as individuals but as a team. Off the floor it is different. Some of the players may not realize my interest in them as individuals at the start, but they later will.

There are plenty of jokes about coaches and character building, but I'm not at UCLA to operate a farm system for the professional league. I'm here as an educator, and I try to teach decency through intercollegiate basketball.[2]

I'm not saying there's no finesse in the pro game, but the college game is mainly finesse, the pro game mainly brute strength.

COACH TAUGHT US SELF-DISCIPLINE AND WAS
ALWAYS HIS OWN BEST EXAMPLE.

—*Kareem Abdul-Jabbar*

I would much rather have my teams overconfident than with a lack of confidence. It is easier to bring a team down to reality than it is to give them confidence.

I never wanted to teach through fear or punishment. I think the greatest motivator is a pat on the back, although I also realize that occasionally the pat must be a little lower and a little harder.

PEOPLE WOULD LOOK AT HIM AND SEE THAT GEN-
TLE SMILE WHICH HELPED DEVELOP THAT IMAGE
OF A MR. NICE GUY, BUT UNDERNEATH THAT SMILE
WAS A KILLER WHO KNEW HOW TO DRIVE HIS
TEAM AND HOW TO GO AFTER THE OTHER TEAM,
BUT ALWAYS WITH A SMILE ON HIS FACE.
—*Walt Hazzard, former player*

I never try to get my players high for a game.
Don't try to psych them up. Don't believe in
it. For every peak there's a valley.[3]

I'm on the boys all the time. I keep telling
them, "You're never any better than your last
game." I hop on them early in the week and
then ease off later in the week. I knock 'em
down and build 'em up.

I told players at UCLA that we, as a team, are like
a powerful car. Maybe a Bill Walton or Kareem
Abdul-Jabbar or Michael Jordan is the big engine,
but if one wheel is flat, we're going no place.[4]

Some of my skeptics, and there have been a few
of my players among them, question whether the
pyramid really accomplishes anything. I can't answer
that. Each person has to answer that for himself. All I
know is that I receive request after request from all
types of organizations to speak about my pyramid. I
do believe it can help everyone to some degree and
certainly can't hurt anyone.[5]

I HAVE THE PYRAMID FRAMED ON MY WALL. I'VE ALWAYS
TRIED TO LIVE BY THEM.[6]

—*Gail Goodrich, former player*

If I could build the ideal coach, I would start with someone who was truly interested in those under his supervision in more reasons than just for their athletic ability.

JOHN WOODEN TOLD ME WHEN I WAS
WORKING AT UCLA, "PLAYERS WIN
GAMES, BUT YOU WANT TO STRIVE TO BE
THE COACH THAT WINS MORE GAMES
WITH HIS PLAYERS THAN SOME OTHER
COACH COACHING YOUR PLAYERS." SO
THAT IS WHAT WE HAVE ALWAYS STRIVED
TO DO—PROVIDE OUR PLAYERS WITH
REAL GOOD COACHING.

—*Dick Vermeil, pro football coach*

7

THE PUPILS

"John Wooden's word is gold."

—CURTIS ROWE

AT UCLA, WHEN I WAS THERE, THE ISSUE WAS NOT
WINNING. THE ISSUE WAS WHO WAS GOING TO GET
TO PLAY THE MOST, THAT'S WHAT WE WERE STRIV-
ING FOR. THE ISSUE OF WINNING WAS A FOREGONE
CONCLUSION IN MOST PEOPLE'S MINDS.[1]

—Lynn Shackelford, former player

COACH WOODEN DOESN'T SEE COLOR.

—Curtis Rowe, former player

IF I HAD GONE TO ANOTHER SCHOOL, I MIGHT
HAVE BEEN A STAND-OUT PLAYER, BUT I'D DO IT
ALL OVER AGAIN. I'M A BETTER PLAYER THANKS TO
COACH WOODEN.[2]

—Larry Farmer, a former player

There's a certain age
when we all test people in
authority. Bill (Walton)
tended to question and
sometimes not with the
most tact, but I knew
his heart was in the
right place.

BILL WALTON SHOWED UP FOR PRACTICE AFTER A
TEN-DAY BREAK WEARING A BEARD, VIOLATING
WOODEN'S RULE OF NO FACIAL HAIR.

"IT'S MY RIGHT," WALTON SAID.

WOODEN ASKED IF HE REALLY BELIEVED THAT
AND WALTON SAID HE DID.

"THAT'S GOOD, BILL. I ADMIRE PEOPLE WHO
HAVE STRONG BELIEFS AND STICK BY THEM. I
REALLY DO, AND WE'RE GOING TO MISS YOU ON
THE TEAM."

WALTON WENT INTO THE LOCKER ROOM AND
SHAVED OFF THE BEARD.

One day Bill Walton came into Wooden's office and told the coach he wanted to try smoking marijuana to reduce the pain in his knees and asked Wooden's permission:

Bill, I haven't heard that it is a pain reliever, but I have heard that it is illegal.[3]

I didn't know if we would have to get (Walton) out of the locker room or out of jail.

I ALWAYS TRIED TO GET COACH WOODEN TO COME TO A GRATEFUL DEAD SHOW WITH ME. HE SAID, "NO, BUT IF YOU'D EVER LIKE TO GO TO A LAWRENCE WELK CONCERT, I'D BE MORE THAN HAPPY TO COME."[4]

—*Bill Walton*

Kareem Abdul-Jabbar and Bill Walton flank their former mentor during a ceremony in which their respective UCLA jerseys were retired. (Photo courtesy of ASUCLA Photography)

WALTON'S ADMIRATION OF WOODEN IS LEGENDARY AND
PART OF THAT RELATIONSHIP ALSO INCLUDES A LITTLE BIT
OF KIDDING AROUND. ONE TIME WALTON WENT UP TO THE
COACH AND SAID, "LET'S GO HAVE A BEER." WOODEN
LOOKED AT WALTON AND QUIETLY REPLIED, "BILL, I'M
EIGHTY-SEVEN AND I HAVEN'T HAD ONE IN MY LIFE. WHY
WOULD I START NOW?"[5]

—Oakland Tribune

Bill (Walton) calls me twice a week and I love talking to him, although it is safe to say, I don't do much of the talking.[6]

You know, when we were playing for Coach Wooden, he was not your friend. He was there to make you better at life. He drove you and he pushed you. But now that I'm old and broken down, we're friends.[7]

—*Bill Walton*

I told him (Kareem Abdul-Jabbar, then known as Lew Alcindor) that I thought he could break Pete Maravich's all-time scoring record, "But if you do, we won't win the NCAA championship every year like I think we can." I told him it was up to him.

HE USED TO CHEW ME OUT IN FRONT OF THE TEAM JUST TO GET ME MAD. HE KNEW I HAD TO BE MAD TO PLAY MY BEST.
—*Walt Hazzard*

HE HAD HIS RULES, AND IF YOU WENT ASTRAY OF THOSE RULES YOU DEFINITELY SUFFERED THE CONSEQUENCES.[8]
—*Mike Warren, former player*

JOHN WOODEN'S WORD IS GOLD.
—*Curtis Rowe*

Almost all my players graduated. Most of them have gone on to great success. I've got doctors, lawyers, teachers, businessmen, and eight ministers.[9]

~

I would tell them education comes first and basketball second. Social activities must come third. You need social activities, but if they come before education or basketball, you'll lose them all.[10]

⌒

COACH WOODEN'S WAYS WOULD STILL WIN TODAY, NO DOUBT. SOME OF MY PLAYERS HAVE SEEN TAPES OF ME PLAYING. I DRIBBLED TO THE POINT, MADE THE PASS, THE BASKET WAS MADE. THEY'D GO, "COACH, YOU HAD NO GAME." MAYBE IT WAS BORING. BUT WE WON WITH IT. WE WON EIGHTY-EIGHT GAMES IN A ROW WITH IT.[11]

—Greg Lee, *former player*

⌒

THE PHILOSOPHY

"A life not lived for others is not a life."
—MOTHER TERESA

Be quick, but don't hurry.

It's not so important who starts the game but who finishes it.

Don't mistake activity for achievement.

I don't like to give suggestions, I like to give opinions.

Be open-minded. There is no progress without change.

Don't let making a living prevent you from making a life.

⌒

The two most important words in life are *love* and *balance*.

⌒

I think those two people have much in common and what they have in common is a consideration for others.
—*on the two people he has admired most,*
Abraham Lincoln and Mother Teresa

⌒

A LIFE NOT LIVED FOR OTHERS IS NOT A LIFE.
—*Mother Teresa*

⌒

THERE'S NOTHING STRONGER THAN GENTLENESS.

—*Abraham Lincoln*

⌒

At times in the public eye, you will be criticized unfairly, and there will be times when the criticism is deserved. You won't like either one.

⌒

Discipline yourself and others won't have to.

⌒

The athlete who says that something cannot be done should never interrupt the one who is doing it.

⌒

Ability may get you to the top, but it takes character to keep you there.

⌒

Nothing will work unless you do.

⌒

Sports do not build character. They reveal it.

⌒

Be more concerned with your character than with your reputation. Your character is what you really are while your reputation is merely what others think you are.

⌒

If you spend too much time learning the tricks of the trade, you may not learn the trade.[1]

⌒

It is best not to drink from a cup full of fame. It can be very intoxicating, and intoxicated people do foolish things.[2]

⌒

What is right is more important than who is right.

~

It is impossible to antagonize and influence at the same time.

~

Things turn out best for those who make the best of the way things turn out.

~

Do not let what you cannot do interfere with what you can do.

~

The greatest joy you can get is saying or doing something that helps another person. That joy is reward in itself.

~

I am not a famous man. I hate being called a wizard. I am not a wizard.[3]

⌒

I think being famous is somebody who did something good for mankind. Mother Teresa was famous. Nobel Prize winners are famous. Basketball coaches aren't famous.

⌒

The most I made coaching at UCLA was $32,500. Maybe I didn't have a million-dollar contract like Shaquille O'Neal, but he'll never know what it was like to get a good meal for twenty-five cents.[4]

⌒

I don't think a man's successful just because he happens to accumulate a lot of material possessions or a position of power and prestige. I think there are other things, and I think it's the other things that bring about the winning that are more important.[5]

⌒

The rolled-up program in hand was a Wooden trademark that he used to get his points across. (Photo courtesy of ASUCLA Photography)

The John Wooden Center is but one part of the coach's great legacy. (Photo courtesy of ASUCLA Photography)

Talent is God-given: be humble. Fame is man-given: be thankful. Conceit is self-given: be careful.[6]

~

You put good fundamentals on a player, you get a good player. You put great fundamentals on a player, you get a great player.

~

Success is peace of mind, which is a direct result of self-satisfaction in knowing you did your best to become the best that you are capable of becoming.

~

In my view, quiet confidence gets the best results. Leaders shouldn't do all the talking. Part of their job is to learn, through listening and observing.

~

Well, hello, Jim. How are you? I'm not really in the market for any insurance these days, but it was kind of you to call. Thank you so much.[7]

—*how Wooden dealt with a telemarketer*

9

THE RETIREMENT

"I felt like I was sitting in on a little bit of sports history."
—MARQUES JOHNSON

I've always told my players to be quick, but don't hurry, but my doctors have told me that I can't fulfill my own advice. I can't be quick or hurry.

—after heart attack in 1972 at age sixty-two

I used to be hanging in. Now I'm hanging on.

I still enjoy coaching. When my enthusiasm wears off, I hope I'll have the sense to retire.

—spoken in 1970

I've always said my first year in coaching was my most satisfying. My last year (1974–75) has been equally satisfying, regardless of what happens Monday night. I've asked J. D. Morgan (UCLA athletic director) to release me from my coaching duties at UCLA.

It's time for younger people to take over.
> —*announcing his retirement at sixty-five after his team beat Louisville in the semifinals of the 1975 NCAA Tournament*

WE WERE JUST GETTING READY TO CELEBRATE WHEN THE MAN WALKED IN AND TOLD US. THE ROOM WENT QUIET. IT WAS A DRAMATIC MOMENT. I FELT LIKE I WAS SITTING IN ON A LITTLE BIT OF SPORTS HISTORY.
> —*Marques Johnson, former player*

I've been accused of making that announcement to fire up my team against Kentucky, but if you have to do something like that to fire up your team to play for the national championship, you're not doing a very good job.

⌒

THIS WAS HIS LAST PREGAME TALK, SO I THOUGHT I'D BETTER LISTEN.

—former player Richard Washington after UCLA's 92 85 victory over Kentucky in the 1975 NCAA Championship, Wooden's last game

⌒

THERE WAS NO WAY WE WERE GOING TO LOSE COACH'S LAST GAME.

—Andre McCarter, former player

⌒

WE WANTED TO WIN IT BAD FOR THE MAN.

—Pete Trgovich, former player

⌒

I don't miss the games at all, and I've never missed the tournament. What I do miss (are) the daily practice sessions, the associations, the preparations.

Yes, I'm sad, sad that I'm leaving the youngsters and all the wonderful associations I've made.

I haven't agreed with you on everything, but we all agree on our love for this game.

—to the media after final game

There's really no pressure in what I'm doing now. If I don't give a good speech, I never hear any jeering.

I won't coach again, ever, but I always hope to be involved in some way with basketball.

I'd do it for nothing. I didn't really want anything, but they insisted I take a little something.

—Wooden at age ninety, after being named a consultant for the American Basketball Association's Los Angeles Stars

THIS IS LIKE WILLIAM SHAKESPEARE ADVISING A LOCAL THEATER, LIKE ALBERT EINSTEIN ADVISING A SCIENCE DEPARTMENT, AND DUKE ELLINGTON ADVISING A LOCAL ORCHESTRA.

—Jamaal Wilkes, vice president of basketball operations for the Stars and former collegiate player for Wooden

10

THE TRIBUTES

*"John Wooden is the greatest
coach ever in any sport."*

—STEVE SPURRIER

The time to make friends is before you need them.

I WISH I COULD BE HALF THE MAN HE IS. I JUST HOPE I CAN
LIVE TO BE NINETY YEARS OLD AND BE ABLE TO IMPACT
PEOPLE'S LIVES LIKE HE HAS.[1]

—*Henry Bibby, former player*

I THINK THE HEAD COACH AT UCLA IS ALWAYS ON THE HOT
SEAT. NO ONE CAN EVER MATCH UP WITH JOHN WOODEN.
MY PREDECESSOR (JIM HARRICK) WON THE NATIONAL
CHAMPIONSHIP ONE YEAR AND THEN STARTED 1-2 THE NEXT
AND THEY WERE CALLING FOR HIS HEAD. I UNDERSTAND
THAT THERE CAN NEVER BE ANOTHER JOHN WOODEN. I JUST
HAVE TO BE MYSELF.

—*current, as of 2001–2002, UCLA coach Steve Lavin*

So many victories and championships, so much hardware. (Photo courtesy of ASUCLA Photography)

COACH WOODEN WILL NEVER BECOME A FOOTNOTE. I CAN
GUARANTEE YOU THAT. ANY PERSON WHO HAS THE CLASS
AND DISTINCTION OF WINNING TEN NATIONAL CHAMPI-
ONSHIPS AND TO DOMINATE A SPORT LIKE NO OTHER
COACH WILL EVER DUPLICATE AGAIN WILL ALWAYS GO
DOWN IN THE ANNALS OF SPORTS HISTORY AS THE
GREATEST OF ALL TIME.

—*Rick Pitino, basketball coach*

IF IT'S FOR COACH WOODEN, WE'LL COME OUT. JUST TELL
ME THE DATE AND TELL ME THE TIME AND WE'LL BE THERE.

—*John Calipari, at the time head coach at Massachusetts,*
when asked if his team would participate in the
inaugural John R. Wooden Classic in California in 1994

I NEVER REALLY APPRECIATED COACH WOODEN UNTIL
AFTER I GOT INTO THE PROS. THEN I REALIZED HE WAS THE
BEST PREPARED COACH I EVER HAD.[2]

—*Keith Erickson, former player*

AS I HAVE GOTTEN OLDER AND LIVED THROUGH MANY OF
LIFE'S ADVENTURES, I HAVE COME TO APPRECIATE COACH
WOODEN EVEN MORE. HE IS ON THE LIST OF PEOPLE WHO
HAVE HAD THE GREATEST IMPACT ON ME. THE SUCCESS HE
ENJOYED IN COACHING IS RARE, BUT COACH WOODEN'S
GIFTS AS A PERSON ARE RARE AS WELL.[3]

—*Kareem Abdul-Jabbar*

I often told my players that, next to my own flesh and
blood, they were the closest to me. They were my
children. I got wrapped up in them, their lives, and
their problems.[4]

TO BE HONEST, I NEVER LOOKED AT JOHN AS A COACH. HE
WAS JUST SUCH A WONDERFUL PERSON TO KNOW. HE WAS
MORE OF A CONFIDANT THAN ANYTHING ELSE. I MEAN, YOU
HAVE TO LISTEN TO SOMEONE LIKE THAT.

—*Jerry West, former L.A. Lakers player and general manager*

JOHN WOODEN IS SO SQUARE HE IS DIVISIBLE BY FOUR.
—*Jim Murray*, Los Angeles Times *columnist*

JOHN WOODEN IS AMERICAN GOTHIC TO THE COLLAR BUT-
TON. YOU MEET HIM AND YOU'RE TEMPTED TO SAY, "ALL
RIGHT, WHAT DID YOU DO WITH THE PITCHFORK, JOHN?"
YOU CAN SMELL THE HAY IF YOU CLOSE YOUR EYES.[5]
—*Jim Murray*

THERE HAS NEVER BEEN ANOTHER COACH LIKE WOODEN,
QUIET AS AN APRIL SNOW AND SQUARE AS A GAME OF
CHECKERS; LOYAL TO ONE WOMAN, ONE SCHOOL, ONE WAY;
WALKING AROUND CAMPUS IN HIS SENSIBLE SHOES AND
JIMMY STEWART MORALS.[6]
—*Rick Reilly*, Sports Illustrated *columnist*

HIS WILLINGNESS TO LISTEN TO THE IDEAS OF OTHERS AND
HIS LACK OF EGO ALLOWED HIM TO CHANGE AND KEEP UP
WITH THE EVER-CHANGING GAME.
—*Denny Crum, an assistant under Wooden at UCLA*

I DON'T THINK ANYBODY WOULD BELIEVE SOMEBODY
COULD WIN SEVEN IN A ROW. I WOULDN'T EITHER. I DON'T
THINK ANYONE CAN DOMINATE LIKE THAT EVER AGAIN. I
DON'T THINK THERE'S BEEN ANYTHING THAT APPROACHES
IT ON A COLLEGE LEVEL. COACH WOODEN WAS
UNEQUALED. I GUESS (RED) AUERBACH WITH THE CELTICS
ON A PROFESSIONAL LEVEL WAS CLOSE. YOU CAN COUNT
COACHES LIKE WOODEN ON ONE HAND.[7]

—Denny Crum

JOHN WOODEN IS THE GREATEST COACH EVER IN ANY SPORT.

*—Steve Spurrier, head football
coach at the University of Florida*

I appreciate the nice things that were said. I'd like
to feel I was deserving, but that would be most
immodest, but it would be unforgivable if I was
not duly appreciative.

A LOT OF KIDS COME IN HERE, EXPECTING TO PLAY TWO
YEARS WITH THEIR INFLATED EGOS, AND THEY DON'T
DEVELOP AS PLAYERS. THEY NEED TO LEARN THE SMALL
THINGS, THE DETAILS. WITH COACH WOODEN, IF YOU
DIDN'T LEARN THESE, YOU DIDN'T PLAY.[8]

—Mike Warren, former player

IT AMAZED ME HOW HE ALWAYS HAD TIME FOR PEOPLE,
EVEN THOSE HE DID NOT KNOW. HE TREATED EVERYONE
WITH THE SAME GENUINE KINDNESS.

—David Meyers, former player

THE PERSON I WAS MOST INTIMIDATED BY DURING THE
COURSE OF AN INTERVIEW WAS JOHN WOODEN. I FELT LIKE I
WAS INTERVIEWING GOD. I WONDERED, WHAT DO I ASK GOD?

—Terry Gannon ABC sportscaster,
who played college basketball at N.C. State

OH, I THOUGHT HE WAS A GOLFER.[9]
> —*former Florida Marlins pitcher Livan Hernandez,*
> *when he saw an interview with Wooden on*
> *television and someone told him why he was famous*

Denny Miller, a former player, was attending a banquet of former UCLA players, when Coach Wooden poked some fun at his former player:
I WAS PLAYING BASKETBALL AT UCLA FOR COACH JOHN WOODEN AND IT WAS IN THE MIDDLE OF MY SENIOR YEAR WHEN I GOT WORD I WAS TO BE TARZAN. MY DAD AND I WENT AND TALKED TO COACH WOODEN AND TOLD HIM HOW SORRY WE WERE THAT I HAD TO LEAVE THE TEAM. BUT COACH WOODEN UNDERSTOOD. HE WAS VERY GRACIOUS ABOUT IT. HE INTRODUCED ME AS THE GUY WHO LEFT THE TEAM TO PLAY TARZAN . . . AND THEN ADDED, "FOR THOSE WHO HAVEN'T SEEN HIS TARZAN MOVIE . . . WELL, YOU DIDN'T MISS ANYTHING."[10]
> —*Denny Miller*

MR. PRESIDENT, YOU BETTER COME OUT HERE, BECAUSE
WORD HAS IT THAT JOHN WOODEN MAY BE OUT HERE TO
GIVE THEM A LITTLE BIT OF AN EDGE. THEY NEED YOU.
*—Chris Fowler, ESPN, April 1, 1995 before the
UCLA-Arkansas NCAA Championship game that year*

WELL, I'M NOWHERE NEAR IN HIS CLASS, BUT I'LL BE
SCREAMING MY LUNGS OUT WHEREVER I AM.
—former president Bill Clinton's reply

I'VE BEEN READING A BOOK THAT EVERYBODY SHOULD READ,
JOHN WOODEN'S BOOK, *REFLECTIONS OF A LIFETIME ON AND
OFF THE COURT*. AND LAST NIGHT, I WAS READING THIS PART
OF IT, HE SAID, YOU KNOW, WHETHER YOU HAVE A FORD OR
A CADILLAC, YOU HAVE TO MAKE IT THE BEST POSSIBLE CAR
OUT THERE RUNNING. AND IT KIND OF HIT ME. I SAID, YOU
KNOW WHAT, MAYBE I AM A FORD RUNNING AGAINST A
BUNCH OF CADILLACS OUT THERE, BUT ALL I CAN DO IS BE
THE BEST FORD I CAN BE. I CAN'T WORRY ABOUT WHAT THE
CADILLACS ARE DOING. I'M AN OLD '67 MUSTANG WITH
VINYL SEATS AND EIGHT-TRACK CASSETTE AND EIGHT-TRACK
PLAYER TRYING TO BEAT UP A BUNCH OF CADILLACS.
—John Maginnes, professional golfer

11

THE GAME TODAY

"I enjoy the game. I'm not sure I enjoy it
as much as I used to. I'm against taunting."

—JOHN WOODEN

IT WOULD BE INTERESTING TO SEE HOW SOME OF TODAY'S
PLAYERS WOULD REACT TO COACH WOODEN. HE EXPECTED
YOU TO BE RESPONSIBLE, TO ARRIVE FOR A SEASON IN
SHAPE, AND TO BE READY TO LEARN. HE EMBRACED THE
IDEA OF TEAM PLAY, SOMETHING THAT HAS REALLY FALLEN
BY THE WAYSIDE.[1]

—*Kareem Abdul-Jabbar*

Good coaching is about leadership and instilling
respect in your players. Dictators lead through fear,
good coaches do not.[2]

It is the responsibility for a leader to inspire those
under your supervision. Coaches are in the public
eye. They are role models, regardless of what Charles
Barkley says.[3]

I don't believe in coaching through fear.

—*referring to Bobby Knight*

⌒

I said some years ago that I was afraid Bobby Knight might self-destruct. The only surprise to me is that it took this long.

—*in 2000, around the time Knight was dismissed from his job as Indiana men's basketball coach*

⌒

The athleticism of current basketball players is unbelievable. The lack of teamwork among the players is also unbelievable.

⌒

I'm very much against showmanship, perhaps more than I should be. I don't like it when they're all by themselves and they do a 360 dunk. That's not necessary. If I want to see showmanship, I'll go see the Globetrotters, and I'll enjoy it.

⌒

Wooden's love for basketball continued well beyond his coaching career. (Photo courtesy of ASUCLA Photography)

If one of my players did a 360 dunk, he would be off the court before his feet hit the floor.

⌒

I do think too much television has been bad for the game, but money rules everything. TV has made actors out of coaches, players, and officials. I wanted my team and its play to be the attraction.

⌒

I think that most adults would say that the happiest days of their lives were their school days. So those who leave college early or go (straight) from high school are missing something that is very important in terms of their total life. I understand the attraction of the big money, but they are missing something vitally important.[4]

⌒

I think the older you get, the more reflective days become, maybe because you have more to reflect about.[5]

⌒

I would rather stay in the background and not take anything away from the team. They had a tremendous season, and I don't want to take any attention away from them. This is their moment. I don't want to get in the way.

—in 1995, after UCLA won its only NCAA basketball championship without him as coach

You aren't here to hear me.

—at the 1994 Wooden Classic after the crowd's third standing ovation for him

They are paid. What's their college education worth?[6]

—when asked if college players should be paid

I enjoy the game. I'm not sure I enjoy it as much as I used to. I'm against taunting. I don't think there's any place for that.[7]

12

THE FAMILY

"The best thing a father can do for his children is to love their mother."

—JOHN WOODEN

I'VE KNOWN A LOT OF MARRIED PEOPLE AND I'VE
ALWAYS SAID WHAT THEY (JOHN AND NELLIE
WOODEN) HAD WAS RARE. IT'S LIKE THEY WERE
ONE PERSON, AND TOTALLY DEVOTED TO EACH
OTHER AND THE FAMILY.

—*Nancy Wooden, daughter*

When I think of Mother, I think of hard
work: cooking, canning, mending, washing on
the washboard, churning our own butter. I
think of perseverance.[1]

My father had a profound influence on
my life. Both my philosophy of life and
of coaching came largely from him.[2]

My father gave me a two-dollar bill for my grade school graduation and said: "Hold onto this and you'll never be broke." A lot of times that's all I've had, but I've never been broke.

My finest personal accomplishment was when Nell said, "I do."[3]

The best thing a father can do for his children is to love their mother.

I could never put my profession before my family or my church. I never bring basketball home.

Being a role model is the most powerful form of educating. Youngsters need good role models more than they need critics. It is one of a parent's greatest responsibilities and opportunities. Too often fathers neglect it because they get so caught up in making a living they forget to make a life.[4]

⌒

People ask if I raised my own family the way I ran the UCLA basketball team. I ran the team pretty much like I ran my family, only with the family I had the greatest co-coach working alongside me by the name of Nellie.[5]

⌒

Nellie wanted to visit Ireland. We were planning to go when I retired but then Nellie wasn't able to.[6]

⌒

I'll never adjust to the loss of Nellie. We were married for fifty-three years. No man ever had a finer wife and mother to his children.

⌒

I'm not afraid to die. Death is my only chance to be with her (Nell) again.

⌒

She (great-granddaughter Cori) started it before I was eighty-nine and wanted to have it ready for my ninetieth birthday. It's photos of all my great-grandchildren. Nothing could ever be more precious to me than this.

⌒

I know I'd rather take a whipping than hear him say a bad word to me.[7]

—on his father, Joshua

⌒

John and Nellie Wooden. (Photo courtesy of ASUCLA Photography)

NOTES

The Indiana Years
1. Associated Press, October 2000.
2. *New Yorker Magazine*, March 22, 1969.
3. Wooden, John, with Jack Tobin, *They Call Me Coach.* Chicago: NTC/Contemporary Publishing Group, 1988, 44.
4. *Los Angeles Times*, February 6, 1969.
5. *Chicago Tribune*, March 5, 1995.
6. Wooden with Tobin, 29.
7. Gould, Todd, *Pioneers of the Hardwood: Indiana and the Birth of Professional Basketball.* Indiana University Press, 1998.
8. John Hareas NBA.com 2000.

The Early Westwood Days
1. Wooden with Tobin, 76.
2. Ibid.
3. Ibid., 104.
4. Ibid., 79.
5. *Los Angeles Times*, March 29, 1989.
6. Wooden, John, with Steve Jamison, *Wooden: A Lifetime of Observations and Reflections on and off the Court.* Chicago: NTC/Contemporary Publishing Group, 1997, 64.

7. Wooden with Tobin, 114.
8. *Sports Illustrated*, 1970.

The Practices

1. *UCLA Magazine*, Spring 2000.
2. *The Sporting News*, April 2001.
3. Wooden with Jamison, 128.
4. Ibid., 132.
5. Ibid., 64.
6. Ibid., 81.
7. Wooden with Tobin, 113.
8. Wooden with Jamison, 60.

The Games

1. *Referee Magazine*, December 1999.
2. *Tampa Tribune*, March 25, 1999.
3. *The Sporting News*, February 9, 1974.

The Dynasty

1. *Sports Illustrated*, November 30, 1970.
2. Chapin, Dwight, and Jeff Prugh, *The Wizard of Westwood*. New York: Warner, 1973.
3. Wooden with Tobin, 15.
4. *St. Petersburg Times*, November 16, 1999.
5. *Athlon Sports Magazine*, Fall 2001.
6. *Sports Illustrated*, December 25, 1972.

The Teacher
1. *UCLA Today Magazine*, October 10, 2000.
2. *Look Magazine*, January 25, 1966.
3. *Los Angeles Times*, March 9, 1972.
4. Wooden with Jamision, 75.
5. Wooden with Tobin, 91.
6. *Beta Theta Pi Magazine*, Fall 2000.

The Pupils
1. *Los Angeles Times*, October 11, 1997.
2. *Daily Bruin*, April 1973.
3. Wooden with Jamison, 93.
4. *The Sporting News*, April 2001.
5. *Oakland Tribune*, May 20, 1998.
6. *Los Angeles Times*, October 14, 2000.
7. *The Sporting News*, April 2001.
8. *Los Angeles Times*, October 11, 1997.
9. *Tampa Tribune*, March 25, 1999.
10. AT&T WorldNet Internet chat, March 23, 2000.
11. Tampa Bay Online.

The Philosophy
1. Wooden with Jamison, 93.
2. Ibid., 71.
3. *Los Angeles Times*, October 14, 2000.
4. *UCLA Magazine*, Spring 2000.
5. *CBS Early Show*, December 13, 2000.
6. Wooden with Jamison, 151.
7. *Los Angeles Times*, March 28, 1998.

The Tributes
1. Irv Kaze on Sports KIEV Radio, October, 14, 2000.
2. *Beta Theta Pi Magazine*, Fall 2000.
3. *New York Times*, December 10, 2000.
4. Wooden with Tobin, p. 62.
5. *Los Angeles Times*, August 10, 1972.
6. *Sports Illustrated*, March 14, 2000.
7. *Athlon Sports Magazine*, Fall 2001.
8. *UCLA's Daily Bruin*, March 2, 2000.
9. Associated Press, April 1, 1999.
10. *Los Angeles Daily News*, June 15, 2001.

The Game Today
1. *New York Times*, December 10, 2000.
2. Lifesplaybook.com.
3. *Abilene Reporter-News*, May 18, 2000.
4. *SportsTravel Magazine*, June 1997.
5. *Seattle Times*, October 14, 1998.
6. AT&T WorldNet Internet chat, March 23, 2000.
7. *Cincinnati Post*, August 4, 1997.

The Family
1. *UCLA Magazine*, Spring 2000.
2. Wooden with Tobin, 25.
3. *Friends Magazine*, March/April 2000.
4. Wooden with Jamison, 19.
5. Ibid., 5.
6. *Friends Magazine*, March/April 2000.
7. *Los Angeles Times*, March 28, 1998.

John Wooden's Game-by-Game Coaching Record at UCLA

(Source: UCLA Men's Basketball 2001–2002 Media Guide)

1948–49 (22–7)

Opponent	Site	Result	Score
Cal-Santa Barbara	Home	W	43–37
Loyola (L.A.)	Home	W	51–38
St. Mary's	San Francisco	W	61–58
San Francisco	San Francisco	W	61–57
Santa Clara	Home	W	61–43
Northwestern	Pan-Pacific	W	49–44
Wisconsin	Pan-Pacific	L	46–49
Washington St.	San Francisco	W	54–44
Stanford	San Francisco	L	47–55
Oregon St.	San Francisco	L	58–62
Stanford	Away	L	52–61
California	Away	W	63–54
USC	Home	W	74–68
USC	Away	L	52–59
Cal Poly	(SLO)	W	68–46
Fresno St.	Home	W	77–33
20th Century-Fox	Home	W	73–55
Pittsburgh	Home	W	51–48
California	Home	W	49–37
Stanford	Home	W	59–48
California	Away	W	45–42
Stanford	Away	W	59–46
Stanford	Home	W	56–50
California	Home	W	59–50
USC	Away	W	51–50
USC	Home	W	63–55
Oregon St.	Away	L	41–53
Oregon St.	Away	W	46–39
Oregon St.	Away	L	35–41

1949–50 (24–7)

Opponent	Site	Result	Score
Arizona St.	Home	W	83–55
San Diego St.	Home	W	65–36
Pepperdine	Home	W	55–41
Santa Clara	San Francisco	W	68–56
San Francisco	San Francisco	L	40–53
Illinois	Away	W	65–63
LaSalle	Away	W	62–57
CCNY	Away	W	60–53
Northwestern	Away	L	58–64
Wisconsin	Away	L	52–54
Marquette	Away	W	68–52
California	Home	W	50–45
Stanford	Home	W	71–55
USC	Away	L	45–58
USC	Home	W	68–47
Cal-Santa Barbara	Home	W	67–43
Cal Poly	(SLO)	W	69–38
Fresno St.	Home	W	93–43
Santa Clara	Home	W	74–64
Stanford	Away	W	65–55
California	Away	W	54–47
Stanford	Home	W	69–59
California	Home	W	64–56
California	Away	W	46–44
Stanford	Away	W	62–57
USC	Home	L	43–45
USC	Away	W	74–57
Washington St.	UCLA	W	60–58
Washington St.	UCLA	W	52–49
Bradley	Kansas City	L	59–73
BYU	Kansas City	L	62–83

1950–51 (19–10)

Opponent	Site	Result	Score
Arizona St.	Home	W	79–49
Oregon	Away	W	77–55
Oregon	Away	L	54–72
Santa Clara	Home	W	71–48
San Jose St.	Home	W	82–59
Bradley	Away	L	74 79
Long Island	NY	L	71–90
Iowa	Away	L	63–80
Pittsburgh	Home	W	68–44
LSU	Home	W	95–66
Stanford	Away	W	78–73
Stanford	Away	L	71–74
USC	Away	L	34–53
USC	Away	W	57–44
Arizona	San Francisco	W	69–63
San Francisco	San Francisco	W	75–42
Cal-Santa Barbara	Home	W	76–55
Pepperdine	Home	W	75–60
California	Away	L	60–62
California	Away	W	61–56
Stanford	Home	W	56–48
Stanford	Home	W	90–67
California	Home	W	75–57
California	Home	W	62–59
USC	Home	W	59–53
USC	Home	L	41–43
USC	Home	W	49–41
Washington	Away	L	51–70
Washington	Away	L	54–71

1951–52 (19–12)

Opponent	Site	Result	Score
Arizona St.	Home	W	85–56
Washington	Away	L	52–60
Washington	Away	L	61–76
San Francisco	Home	W	64–55
West Texas St.	Home	W	64–57
Denver	Home	W	60–58
Denver	Home	W	60–51
Kentucky	Away	L	53–84
Illinois	Away	L	67–73
Bradley	Away	W	67–66
Stanford	Home	W	81–63
Stanford	Home	L	71–73
USC	Away	W	55–48
USC	Away	W	67–58
California	Away	L	59–61
California	Away	L	51–54
St. Mary's	San Francisco	W	70–62
Santa Clara	San Francisco	L	59–66
Pepperdine	Home	W	72–70
Cal Poly	SLO	W	67–40
Stanford	Away	W	72–68
Stanford	Away	L	68–77
California	Home	W	67–54
California	Home	W	68–42
USC	Home	W	66–51
USC	Home	W	63–57
Washington	UCLA	W	65–53
Washington	UCLA	L	50–53
Washington	UCLA	W	60–50
Santa Clara	Corvallis, OR	L	59–68
Oklahoma City	Corvallis, OR	L	53–55

1952–53 (16–8)

Opponent	Site	Result	Score
Oregon St.	Away	W	73–63
Oregon St.	Away	W	58–43
Washington	Home	L	49–53
Washington	Home	W	54–47
Michigan St.	Away	W	60–55
Notre Dame	East Lansing, MI	L	60–68
Bradley	Away	W	91–83
Oregon St.	Home	W	74–58
Oregon St.	Home	W	69–61
California	Home	L	68–72
California	Home	L	66–68
USC	Home	L	54–65
USC	Home	W	72–62
Stanford	Away	W	67–66
Stanford	Away	W	74–71
San Diego St.	Home	W	77–48
Bradley	Home	W	79–73
Cal-Santa Barbara	Home	W	91–50
California	Away	W	67–63
California	Away	L	62–70
Stanford	Home	W	75–50
Stanford	Home	W	66–58
USC	Away	L	65–66
USC	Away	L	64–76

1953–54 (18–7)

Opponent	Site	Result	Score
West Texas St.	Home	W	79–48
Arizona	Home	W	90–45
Arizona	Home	W	84–48
Denver	Away	W	70–63
Denver	Away	W	66–45
LaSalle	Lexington, KY	L	53–62
Duke	Lexington, KY	W	72–67
Oregon	Home	W	89–74
Oregon	Home	W	79–53
Iowa	Pan-Pacific	L	60–65
Michigan St.	Pan-Pacific	W	67–57
California	Away	L	53–62
California	Away	L	65–73
USC	Away	L	65–68
USC	Away	W	81–63
Oregon	Home	W	66–56
Pepperdine	Home	W	103–68
Stanford	Home	W	92–73
Stanford	Home	W	77–58
California	Home	W	82–54
California	Home	W	71–62
Stanford	Away	W	92–77
Stanford	Away	W	88–80
USC	Home	L	68–79
USC	Home	L	67–69

1954–55 (21–5)

Opponent	Site	Result	Score
Kansas St.	Home	W	86–57
Santa Clara	Home	W	74–39
San Francisco	Home	W	47–40
Santa Clara	Away	W	65–58
San Francisco	Away	L	44–56
Colorado	Home	W	65–62
New Mexico	Home	W	106–41
Niagara	NY	W	88–86
LaSalle	NY	L	77–85
Dayton	NY	W	104–92
Stanford	Away	L	56–61
Stanford	Away	W	91–75
USC	Home	W	70–67
USC	Home	W	76–64
Cal-Santa Barbara	Home	W	91–62
Cal Poly	SLO	W	84–55
California	Home	W	83–64
California	Home	W	84–63
Stanford	Home	W	85–63
Stanford	Home	W	72–59
California	Away	W	55–48
California	Away	W	84–76
USC	Long Beach	W	66–65
USC	Long Beach	W	75–55
Oregon St.	Corvallis, OR	L	75–82
Oregon St.	Corvallis, OR	L	64–83

1955–56 (22–6)

Opponent	Site	Result	Score
BYU	Away	L	58–75
BYU	Away	L	65–67
Denver	Long Beach	W	68–40
Purdue	Long Beach	W	76–60
Nebraska	Away	L	65–71
Wichita St.	Away	L	68–76
St. John's	NY	W	93–86
Duquesne	NY	W	72–57
San Francisco	NY	L	53–70
Idaho	Pan-Pacific	W	92–73
Idaho	Pan-Pacific	W	78–61
Washington St.	Away	W	86–72
Washington St.	Away	W	95–70
Arizona St.	Away	W	99–79
Washington	Pan-Pacific	W	61–60
Washington	Pan-Pacific	W	82–75
Stanford	Away	W	50–48
Stanford	Away	W	81–72
Oregon St.	Away	W	77–56
Oregon St.	Away	W	72–59
Oregon	Venice	W	95–71
Oregon	Venice	W	108–89
California	Venice	W	85–80
California	Venice	W	84–62
USC	Venice	W	85–70
USC	Loyola	W	97–84
San Francisco	Corvallis, OR	L	61–72
Seattle	Corvallis, OR	W	94–70

1956–57 (22–4)

Opponent	Site	Result	Score
Nebraska	Home	W	69–56
Nebraska	Home	W	78–60
Santa Clara	Bakersfield	W	60–58
BYU	Home	W	74–69
BYU	Home	L	58–59
Missouri	Home	W	77–54
Occidental	Home	W	93–40
St. Louis	Away	W	72–66
Butler	Away	W	82–71
Indiana	Away	W	52–48
Idaho	Away	W	64–63
Idaho	Away	W	69-68
Washington St.	Home	W	87–65
Washington St.	Home	W	83–62
Oregon St.	Long Beach	W	59–37
Oregon St.	Long Beach	W	64–53
Washington	Away	W	68–65
Washington	Away	L	74–90
Stanford	Home	W	86–63
Stanford	Home	W	79–61
Oregon	Away	W	81–62
Oregon	Away	W	73–65
USC	Home	L	80–84
California	Away	W	71–66
California	Away	L	68–73
USC	Home	W	65–55

1957–58 (16–10)

Opponent	Site	Result	Score
St. Mary's	Home	W	70–64
Oklahoma	Home	W	65–53
DePauw	Home	W	82–52
DePauw	Home	W	73–48
Wichita State	Away	L	68–83
Bradley	Away	L	43–67
Evansville	Away	L	76–83
Michigan St.	Home	L	61–63
Ohio State	Home	W	98–78
Oregon	Away	W	64–58
Oregon St.	Away	L	61–68
Oregon	Home	W	73–64
Idaho	Home	W	64–56
USC	Home	W	52–51
USC	Home	W	80–75
Santa Clara	Bakersfield	W	77–56
Washington St.	Home	W	72–64
California	Home	L	58–61
Washington St.	Away	W	64–44
Idaho	Away	L	67–73
Washington	Away	W	67–62
Stanford	Long Beach	W	46–43
Oregon St.	Long Beach	L	61–77
California	Away	L	50–56
Stanford	Away	L	50–57
Washington	UCLA	W	89–68

1958–59 (16–9)

Opponent	Site	Result	Score
St. Mary's	San Francisco	L	59–62
Santa Clara	San Francisco	L	42–56
Kansas	Home	W	72–61
Iowa State	Home	W	65–63
Colorado	Home	W	58–48
Colorado	Home	W	56–54
Santa Clara	Home	L	47–49
Denver	Home	W	71–57
Idaho	Away	W	62–53
Washington St.	Away	L	54–71
Washington	Away	L	63–68
Washington St.	Home	W	68–41
Oregon St.	Home	W	73–62
USC	Home	W	57–53
USC	Home	W	65–63
Cal-Santa Barbara	UCLA	W	63–59
California	Home	L	58–60
Idaho	Home	L	87–91
Stanford	Away	L	61–69
California	Away	L	51–64
Oregon	Home	W	70–53
Stanford	Home	W	64–51
Oregon St.	Away	W	71–59
Oregon	Away	W	69–62
Washington	UCLA	W	56–55

1959–60 (14–12)

Opponent	Site	Result	Score
USC	Home	W	47–45
Kentucky	Home	L	66–68
Santa Clara	Home	W	75–73
BYU	Home	W	62–42
Oklahoma St.	Home	L	48–52
Purdue	Away	L	74–75
Butler	Away	L	73–79
Minnesota	Away	W	73–72
Michigan	Home	W	93–68
West Virginia	Home	L	73–87
USC	Home	L	62–72
Washington	Home	W	57–55
Washington	Home	W	55–54
California	Away	L	47–59
USC	Home	W	63–62
Denver	Away	L	68–71
Air Force	Away	W	76–75
New Mexico St.	Home	W	66–56
Stanford	Home	W	67–54
Stanford	Away	W	58–52
California	Away	L	45–53
Stanford	Home	W	49–48
California	Home	L	57–67
Washington	Away	L	73–84
USC	Home	L	71–91
USC	Home	W	72–70

1960–61 (18–8)

Opponent	Site	Result	Score
Oklahoma St.	Away	L	58–64
Tulsa	Away	W	94–74
Kansas St.	Home	W	83–73
NYU	Home	W	93–69
Notre Dame	Home	W	85–54
Butler	Home	W	73–61
Michigan St.	Home	W	98–61
Indiana	Home	W	94–72
Iowa	Home	L	65–71
Washington	Away	L	45–58
Washington	Away	W	62–58
Arizona	Home	W	90–68
California	Home	W	54–46
Denver	Home	W	85–64
Air Force	Home	W	89–78
USC	Home	L	63–78
USC	Home	W	86–83
Stanford	Away	L	65–79
Kentucky	Away	L	76–77
Loyola	Chicago	W	87–82
California	Away	L	65–66
Stanford	Away	W	70-56
USC	Home	L	85-86
Washington	Home	W	84-58
Stanford	Home	W	69-55
California	Home	W	59-55

1961–62 (18–11)

Opponent	Site	Result	Score
BYU	Away	L	66–68
BYU	Away	L	83–86
Kansas	Home	W	69–61
DePauw	Home	W	91–62
Colorado St.	Home	L	68–69
Creighton	Away	L	72–74
Houston	Away	L	65–91
Texas A&M	Houston	W	81–71
Army	Home	W	86–72
Ohio State	Home	L	84–105
Utah	Home	L	79–88
Washington	Home	W	72–57
Washington	Home	W	75–63
California	Away	W	71–60
Texas Tech	Santa Monica	W	89–60
Texas Tech	Santa Monica	W	87–58
USC	Home	W	73–59
Stanford	Santa Monica	W	82–64
USC	Home	L	60–74
USC	Home	W	69–62
California	Home	W	68–62
Stanford	Home	W	75–65
Washington	Away	W	69–66
Stanford	Away	L	67–82
California	Away	W	66–54
Utah St.	Provo	W	73–62
Oregon St.	Provo	W	88–69
Cincinnati	Louisville	L	70–72
Wake Forest	Louisville	L	80–82

1962–63 (20–9)

Opponent	Site	Result	Score
Denver	Home	W	70–41
Santa Clara	UCLA	W	66–41
Colorado	Away	L	60–82
Colorado St.	Away	L	65–66
Oklahoma	Santa Monica	W	101–64
Missouri	Santa Monica	W	72–55
Butler	Away	W	81–68
Northwestern	Away	W	70–63
Wisconsin	Away	W	77–63
Utah St.	Home	W	89–75
St. Louis	Home	W	85–66
Colorado St.	Home	W	68–64
Washington	Away	L	61–62
Washington	Away	L	63–67
California	Santa Monica	W	63–58
Texas Tech	Away	W	83–63
Texas Tech	Away	W	103–80
USC	Home	W	77–65
USC	Home	W	86–72
Stanford	Away	L	78–86
Stanford	Away	L	69–73
California	Away	W	64–57
USC	Home	L	60–62
Washington	Santa Monica	W	80–52
Stanford	Santa Monica	W	64–54
California	Santa Monica	W	72–53
Stanford	Santa Monica	W	51–45
Arizona St.	Provo	L	79–93
San Francisco	Provo	L	75–76

1963–64 (30–0)
National Champions

Opponent	Site	Result	Score
BYU	Home	W	113–71
Butler	Home	W	80–65
Kansas St.	Lawrence, KS	W	78–75
Kansas	Manhattan, KS	W	74–54
Baylor	Long Beach	W	112–61
Creighton	Long Beach	W	95–79
Yale	Home	W	95–65
Michigan	Home	W	98–80
Illinois	Home	W	83–79
Washington St.	Away	W	88–83
Washington St.	Away	W	121–77
USC	Home	W	79–59
USC	Home	W	78–71
Stanford	Home	W	84–71
Stanford	Santa Monica	W	80–61
Cal-Santa Barbara	Away	W	107–76
Cal-Santa Barbara	Santa Monica	W	87–59
California	Away	W	87–67
California	Away	W	58–56
Washington	Home	W	73–58
Washington	Home	W	88–60
Stanford	Away	W	100–88
Washington	Away	W	78–64
Washington St.	Home	W	93–56
California	Home	W	87–57
USC	Home	W	91–81
Seattle	Corvallis, OR	W	95–90
San Francisco	Corvallis, OR	W	76–72
Kansas St.	Kansas City	W	90–84
Duke	Kansas City	W	98–83

1964–65 (28–2)
National Champions

Opponent	Site	Result	Score
Illinois	Away	L	83–110
Indiana St.	Away	W	112–76
Arizona St.	Home	W	107–76
Oklahoma St.	Home	W	68–52
Marquette	Milwaukee	W	61–52
Boston College	Milwaukee	W	115–93
USC	Home	W	84–75
Arizona	Home	W	99–79
Minnesota	Home	W	93–77
Utah	Home	W	104–74
Oregon	Away	W	91–74
Oregon St.	Away	W	83–53
California	Home	W	76–54
Stanford	Home	W	80–66
Iowa	Chicago	L	82–87
Loyola	Chicago	W	85–72
Washington St.	Home	W	93–41
Washington	Home	W	78–75
Washington	Away	W	83–73
Washington St.	Away	W	70–68
Oregon St.	Home	W	73–55
Oregon	Home	W	74–64
Stanford	Away	W	83–67
California	Away	W	83–68
USC	Home	W	77–71
USC	Home	W	52–50
BYU	Provo	W	100–76
San Francisco	Provo	W	101–93
Wichita St.	Portland	W	108–89
Michigan	Portland	W	91–80

1965–66 (18–8)

Opponent	Site	Result	Score
Ohio State	Home	W	92–66
Illinois	Home	W	97–79
Duke	Durham	L	66–82
Duke	Charlotte	L	75–94
Kansas	Home	W	78–71
Cincinnati	Sports Arena	L	76–82
USC	Sports Arena	W	86–67
LSU	Sports Arena	W	95–89
Purdue	Sports Arena	W	82–70
USC	Sports Arena	W	94–76
Oregon St.	Home	W	79–35
Oregon	Home	W	97–65
California	Away	W	75–66
Stanford	Away	L	69–74
Loyola	Chicago	L	96–102
Arizona	Home	W	84–67
Washington St.	Away	L	83–84
Washington	Away	W	89–67
Washington St.	Home	W	88–61
Washington	Home	W	100–71
Oregon St.	Away	L	51–64
Oregon	Away	L	72–79
California	Home	W	95–79
Stanford	Home	W	70–58
USC	Home	W	94–79
USC	Sports Arena	W	99–62

1966–67 (30–0)
National Champions

Opponent	Site	Result	Score
USC	Home	W	105–90
Duke	Home	W	88–54
Duke	Home	W	107–87
Colorado St.	Home	W	84–74
Notre Dame	Home	W	96–67
Wisconsin	Home	W	100–56
Georgia Tech	Home	W	91–72
USC	Home	W	107–83
Washington St.	Away	W	76–67
Washington	Away	W	83–68
California	Home	W	96–78
Stanford	Home	W	116–78
Portland	Home	W	122–57
Cal-Santa Barbara	Home	W	119–75
Loyola	Chicago	W	82–67
Illinois	Chicago	W	120–82
USC	Sports Arena	W (OT)	40–35
Oregon St.	Home	W	76–44
Oregon	Home	W	100–66
Oregon	Away	W	34–25
Oregon St.	Away	W	72–50
Washington	Home	W	71–43
Washington St.	Home	W	100–78
Stanford	Away	W	75–47
California	Away	W	103–66
USC	Home	W	83–55
Wyoming	Corvallis, OR	W	109–69
Pacific	Corvallis, OR	W	80–64
Houston	Louisville	W	73–58
Dayton	Louisville	W	79–64

1967–68 (29–1)
National Champions

Opponent	Site	Result	Score
Purdue	Away	W	73–71
Wichita St.	Home	W	120–86
Iowa State	Home	W	121–80
Bradley	Home	W	109–73
Notre Dame	Home	W	114–63
Minnesota	Sports Arena	W	95–55
St. Louis	Sports Arena	W	108–67
Wyoming	Sports Arena	W	104–71
Washington St.	Home	W	97–69
Washington	Home	W	93–65
California	Away	W	94–64
Stanford	Away	W	75–63
Portland	Home	W	93–69
Houston	Astrodome	L	69–71
Holy Cross	NY	W	90–67
Boston College	NY	W	84–77
USC	Home	W	101–67
Oregon St.	Away	W	55–52
Oregon	Away	W	104–63
Oregon	Home	W	119–78
Oregon St.	Home	W	88–71
Washington	Away	W	84–64
Washington St.	Away	W	101–70
Stanford	Home	W	100–62
California	Home	W	115–71
USC	Sports Arena	W	72–64
New Mexico St.	Albuquerque	W	58–49
Santa Clara	Albuquerque	W	87–66
Houston	Sports Arena	W	101–69
North Carolina	Sports Arena	W	78–55

1968–69 (29–1)
National Champions

Opponent	Site	Result	Score
Purdue	Home	W	94–82
Ohio State	Away	W	84–73
Notre Dame	Away	W	88–75
Minnesota	Home	W	90–51
West Virginia	Home	W	95–56
Providence	NY	W	98–81
Princeton	NY	W	83–67
St. John's	NY	W	74–56
Tulane	Home	W	96–64
Oregon	Away	W	93–64
Oregon St.	Away	W	83–64
Houston	Home	W	100–64
Northwestern	Away	W	81–67
Loyola	Chicago	W	84–65
California	Home	W	109–74
Stanford	Home	W	98–61
Washington	Home	W	62–51
Washington St.	Home	W	108–80
Washington St.	Away	W	83–59
Washington	Away	W	53–44
Oregon St.	Home	W	91–66
Oregon	Home	W	103–69
Stanford	Away	W	81–60
California	Away	W	84–77
USC	Sports Arena	W	61–55
USC	Home	L	44–46
New Mexico St.	UCLA	W	53–38
Santa Clara	UCLA	W	90–52
Drake	Louisville	W	85–82
Purdue	Louisville	W	92–72

1969–70 (28–2)
National Champions

Opponent	Site	Result	Score
Arizona	Home	W	90–65
Minnesota	Away	W	72–71
Miami	Home	W	127–69
LSU	Home	W	133–84
Texas	Home	W	99–54
Georgia Tech	Home	W	121–90
Princeton	Home	W	76–75
Notre Dame	Home	W	108–77
Oregon	Home	W	75–58
Oregon St.	Home	W	72–71
Bradley	Chicago	W	61–58
Loyola	Chicago	W	94–72
Cal-Santa Barbara	Home	W	89–80
Wyoming	Home	W	115–77
California	Away	W	87–72
Stanford	Away	W	102–84
Washington	Away	W	66–56
Washington St.	Away	W	72–70
Washington St.	Home	W	95–61
Washington	Home	W	101–85
Oregon St.	Away	W	71–56
Oregon	Away	L	65–78
Stanford	Home	W	120–90
California	Home	W	109–95
USC	Home	L	86–87
USC	Sports Arena	W	91–78
CSLB	Seattle	W	88–65
Utah State	Seattle	W	101–79
New Mexico St.	College Park, MD	W	93–77
Jacksonville	College Park, MD	W	80–69

1970–71 (29–1)
National Champions

Opponent	Site	Result	Score
Baylor	Home	W	108–77
Rice	Home	W	124–78
Pacific	Home	W	100–88
Tulsa	Home	W	95–75
Missouri	Home	W	94–75
St. Louis	Home	W	79–65
William&Mary	Pittsburgh	W	90–71
Pittsburgh	Pittsburgh	W	77–65
Dayton	Home	W	106–82
Washington	Home	W	78–69
Washington St.	Home	W	95–71
Stanford	Away	W	58–53
California	Away	W	94–76
Loyola	Chicago	W	87–62
Notre Dame	Away	L	82–89
Cal-Santa Barbara	Home	W	74–61
USC	Sports Arena	W	64–60
Oregon	Away	W	69–68
Oregon St.	Away	W	67–65
Oregon St.	Home	W	94-64
Oregon	Home	W	74–67
Washington St.	Away	W	57–53
Washington	Away	W	71–69
California	Home	W	103–69
Stanford	Home	W	107–72
USC	Home	W	73–62
BYU	Utah	W	91–73
CSLB	Utah	W	57–55
Kansas	Houston	W	68–60
Villanova	Houston	W	68–62

1971–72 (30–0)
National Champions

Opponent	Site	Result	Score
The Citadel	Home	W	105–49
Iowa	Home	W	106–72
Iowa State	Home	W	110–81
Texas A&M	Home	W	117–53
Notre Dame	Home	W	114–56
TCU	Home	W	119–81
Texas	Home	W	115–65
Ohio State	Home	W	79–53
Oregon St.	Away	W	78–72
Oregon	Away	W	93–68
Stanford	Home	W	118–79
California	Home	W	82–43
Santa Clara	Home	W	92–57
Denver	Home	W	108–61
Loyola	Chicago	W	92–64
Notre Dame	Away	W	57–32
USC	Home	W	81–56
Washington St.	Home	W	89–58
Washington	Home	W	109–70
Washington	Away	W	100–83
Washington St.	Away	W	85–55
Oregon	Home	W	92–70
Oregon St.	Home	W	91–72
California	Away	W	85–71
Stanford	Away	W	102–73
USC	Sports Arena	W	79–66
Weber St.	Provo	W	90–58
CSLB	Provo	W	73–57
Louisville	Sports Arena	W	96–77
Florida St.	Sports Arena	W	81–76

1972–73 (30–0)
National Champions

Opponent	Site	Result	Score
Wisconsin	Home	W	94–53
Bradley	Home	W	73–38
Pacific	Home	W	81–48
Cal-Santa Barbara	Home	W	98–67
Pittsburgh	Home	W	89–73
Notre Dame	Home	W	82–56
Drake	New Orleans	W	85–72
Illinois	New Orleans	W	71–64
Oregon	Home	W	64–38
Oregon St.	Home	W	87–61
Stanford	Away	W	82–67
California	Away	W	69–50
San Francisco	Home	W	92–64
Providence	Home	W	101–77
Loyola	Chicago	W	87–73
Notre Dame	Away	W	82–63
USC	Sports Arena	W	79–56
Washington St.	Away	W	88–50
Washington	Away	W	76–67
Washington	Home	W	93–62
Washington St.	Home	W	96–64
Oregon	Away	W	72–61
Oregon St.	Away	W	73–67
California	Home	W	90–65
Stanford	Home	W	51–45
USC	Home	W	76–56
Arizona St.	UCLA	W	98–81
San Francisco	UCLA	W	54–39
Indiana	St. Louis	W	70–59
Memphis St.	St. Louis	W	87–66

1973–74 (26–4)

Opponent	Site	Result	Score
Arkansas	Home	W	101–79
Maryland	Home	W	65–64
SMU	Home	W	77–60
N.C. State	St. Louis	W	84–66
Ohio U.	Home	W	110–63
St. Bonaventure	Home	W	111–59
Wyoming	Home	W	86–58
Michigan	Home	W	90–70
Washington	Away	W	100–48
Washington St.	Away	W	55–45
California	Home	W	92–56
Stanford	Home	W	66–52
Iowa	Chicago	W	68–44
Notre Dame	Away	L	70–71
Santa Clara	Home	W	96–54
Notre Dame	Home	W	94–75
USC	Home	W	65–54
Oregon	Home	W	84–66
Oregon St.	Home	W	80–75
Oregon St.	Away	L	57-61
Oregon	Away	L	51–56
Washington St.	Home	W	93–68
Washington	Home	W	99–65
California	Oakland	W	83–60
Stanford	Away	W	62–60
USC	Sports Arena	W	82–52
Dayton	Tucson	W (3-OT)	111–100
San Francisco	Tucson	W	83–60
N.C. State	Greensboro	L (2-OT)	77–80
Kansas	Greensboro	W	78–61

1974–75 (28–3)
National Champions

Opponent	Site	Result	Score
Wichita St.	Home	W	85–74
DePaul	Home	W	79–64
Loyola (Chicago)	Home	W	84–67
Oklahoma St.	Home	W	82–51
Memphis St.	Home	W	113–94
Notre Dame	Home	W	85–72
St. Bonaventure	Maryland	W	78–62
Maryland	Away	W	81–75
Davidson	Home	W	91–64
Oklahoma	Home	W	111–66
Washington	Home	W	92–82
Washington St.	Home	W	77–69
Stanford	Away	L	60–64
California	Away	W	102–72
Cal-Santa Barbara	Home	W	104–76
Notre Dame	Away	L	78–84
USC	Home	W	89–84
Oregon St.	Away	W	67–60
Oregon	Away	W	107–103
Oregon	Home	W	96-66
Oregon St.	Home	W	74-62
Washington St.	Away	W	69–61
Washington	Away	L	81–103
California	Home	W	51–47
Stanford	Home	W	93–59
USC	Away	W	72–68
Michigan	Pullman, WA	W (OT)	103–91
Montana	Portland	W	67–64
Arizona St.	Portland	W	89–75
Louisville	San Diego	W (OT)	75–74
Kentucky	San Diego	W	92–85